Bedrooms

COUNTRY LIVING
EASY TRANSFORMATIONS

Bedrooms

Janice Easton-Epner

HEARST BOOKS
A Division of Sterling Publishing Co., Inc.
New York

A Primrose Productions Book
Designed by Stephanie Stislow

The Library of Congress has cataloged the hardcover edition as follows:
Easton-Epner, Janice.
    Country living : easy transformations, bedrooms / Janice Easton-Epner.
        p. cm.
    Includes Index.
    ISBN 1-58816-452-7
1. Interior decoration. 2. Bedrooms. I. Title.
    NK2117.B4E18 2005
    747.7'7—dc22

                                        2004030048

10 9 8 7 6 5 4 3 2 1

First Paperback Edition 2007
Published by Hearst Books
A Division of Sterling Publishing Co., Inc.
387 Park Avenue South, New York, NY 10016

Country Living and Hearst Books are trademarks of Hearst Communications, Inc.

www.countryliving.com

For information about custom editions, special sales, premium and corporate purchases, please contact Sterling Special Sales Department at 800-805-5489 or specialsales@sterlingpub.com.

Distributed in Canada by Sterling Publishing
c/o Canadian Manda Group, 165 Dufferin Street
Toronto, Ontario, Canada M6K 3H6

Distributed in Australia by Capricorn Link (Australia) Pty. Ltd.
P.O. Box 704, Windsor, NSW 2756 Australia

Manufactured in China

Sterling ISBN 13: 978-1-58816-575-6
     ISBN 10: 1-58816-575-2

Contents

Foreword

Bedrooms play an important role in our lives. They are where we greet each day and where we wind down every evening. Choosing a decorating scheme that embodies both serenity and personal style is essential to our wellbeing. Because bedrooms are such intimate spaces, they are the perfect spots to use favorite colors, patterns, and accessories. I love to display collections like McCoy vases in my bedroom. Not only are these cherished pieces beautiful to look at, they also trigger fond memories of when I found them.

Figuring out where to begin can be tricky. Fortunately, *Country Living Easy Transformations: Bedrooms* takes the guesswork out of the process. The following pages are filled with lovely bedrooms to inspire you. Helpful advice throughout the book addresses both practical concerns (how to pick the best mattress, pillow, and comforter) as well as purely decorative ones (how to create the illusion of a canopy without buying a new bed). Whether you envision a romantic hideaway or a cheerful country nest, you'll find lots of great ideas for achieving the look you want quickly and inexpensively. Sweet dreams!

NANCY MERNIT SORIANO
Editor-in-Chief
Country Living

LEFT: A pillow featuring Victorian-style silhouettes in black-and-white provides a dramatic focal point for this bedroom.

Introduction

In medieval times, there were clear distinctions between the public and private areas of royal castles. The public areas were grandiose, meant to intimidate the visitor into awe at the owner's power. The private areas, by no means less impressive, were decorated not only to suit the royal taste but also so that those few invited in would feel they enjoyed a special access to the room's owner. While modern designers have abandoned many of the traditional formal distinctions between public and private, the bedroom does retain a special role as a private area into which we invite only a select few. As a result, decorating the bedroom poses some unique creative challenges. This book is designed to walk you through the process of transforming an uninspiring bedroom into the bedroom of your dreams.

The first (and most important) considerations are the private ones. Above all, the bedroom should be a space in which you can comfortably relax and sleep. Think carefully about what kind of surroundings help you to feel most relaxed. In what environments have you slept best in the past? Take some time to answer this question— what you learn will help you to create a bedroom that becomes a personal sanctuary and a place where you can reliably come to wind down and get restful sleep.

Next, consider what other roles your bedroom might need to play. Perhaps you would also like it to be a romantic or sensuous space, a room in which you can luxuriate and pamper yourself. Or perhaps you long for a quiet, private haven where you can read and reflect. You might need your bedroom to double as a home office or want to include a separate media center apart from the rest of the house. The bedroom may also be a storage spot (though you should never treat it as a place to toss furniture or clutter that doesn't fit in the public areas of your home). Any of these requirements, from the practical to the indulgent, can be accommodated, but it is important not to let them take precedence over getting a good night's sleep.

If there is too much furniture or clothing in the room, you will feel cramped, and it will be difficult to get a good night's sleep. Likewise, too many electronics—television, computer, stereo, etc.—will be overstimulating unless they can be hidden away at night so you won't be tempted to watch late-night television into the wee hours of the morning. In general, a cluttered or cramped room is not a tranquil place. As you look at your space, simply keep in mind that you will want to create a balance in the room that favors relaxation over other activities.

Start by listing the major pieces of furniture that you will be including. Obviously, the bed is of primary importance! How big is it? Where do you want it? Will you need night tables placed nearby? Other likely furnishings may include a dresser, armoires to hold clothing or electronics, seating (for one or several), a desk or other table, and shelving for personal items, objets d'art or books. Once your list is assembled, you can start to picture the placement for each item—this imaginative exercise will help you achieve the right balance. If you are getting a sense that the room will be cluttered, rethink your needs; perhaps you don't really need all these items in your bedroom. On the other hand, if things seem to be coming together nicely, it's time to move on to the really fun part of decorating your room.

With the question of balance resolved, you are ready to think about the personal expression you want for your room. Now is the time to consider style, color, patterns, fabrics, lighting, and details. Do you dream of a cozy cottage-style bedroom with a romantic bed and floral linens? Or perhaps you've always longed for a colorful, sensuous boudoir? Maybe your perfect bedroom is a spare, Zen-influenced sanctuary? Or it may be that your ideal bedroom is an eclectic mix of periods or styles, filled with items that hold special meaning for you. Whatever your desires, *Country Living Easy Transformations: Bedrooms* has ideas to inspire you, whether you are aiming toward a period-style bedroom, a sleek contemporary sleeping area, or a romantic retreat.

And when your own room has been transformed, you may want to start thinking about how to make your guest room just as inviting—here are plenty of great ideas for those bedrooms as well. Also included are handy tips for solving minor problems or making quick changes, from soundproofing your bedroom to crafting a custom headboard. With its mix of practical suggestions and inspiring ideas, *Country Living Easy Transformations: Bedrooms* will help you to transform any bedroom into a haven of relaxation and enjoyment.

Small Changes, Big Results

You may not be ready for a complete redecoration of your bedroom, whether for reasons of time, budget, or convenience—yet you'd still like to make a change to give the room a fresh look. Here are some ideas for minor alterations that can make a big difference. A new look does not have to be costly. First, look around the room to reassess your current possessions and determine which can be kept, which altered, and which really must go. Perhaps you (or your partner) have a sentimental attachment to a particular piece; it need not be a deterrent to change. The key to any transformation, no matter the magnitude, is to look at your bedroom with a critical eye. Perhaps all your room needs is a fresh coat of paint, new bed linens, a collection of colorful decorative pillows on the bed, or a rearrangement of the furniture.

Settle on the items that are going to stay and use them as a launch pad for your new décor. Think about the ambience you'd like to achieve and consider the role each element—furnishings, color scheme, accessories, lighting—could play in achieving your goals. Then you can begin to edit and add with enthusiasm. Remember, your bedroom doesn't need to fit anyone else's idea of fashionable; rather, it should be filled with things you love.

The rooms in this chapter don't fall neatly into any particular style. What they share is an atmosphere of ease and relaxation, a feeling of comfort that you, too, can create with a little bit of effort. Let them inspire you to try some small changes that may make a big difference!

LEFT: Focusing on a particular color is a wonderful way to change the feeling of a room. Here, it is pink that defines the room. Pink walls create a warm and comforting backdrop. Repeating the color in different shades adds depth throughout the room, as with the pale pink of the bench at the foot of the bed and the flowers on the sheets and duvet cover. A button-tufted headboard adds a more modern touch to the cottage ambience.

RIGHT: A big bedroom gets a simple but effective makeover with a coat of blue paint and new bed linens in a mix of patterns. Resisting the urge to cram a lot of furniture into the space allows the elegant pieces to stand out and gives the room a sense of spaciousness and tranquillity. Blue is considered a soothing color; here the subdued tones of the walls and bedclothes contribute to the calm atmosphere. New toile de Jouy window shades add a country air.

NOTE HOW THE CURVES OF THE BUREAU AND THE CHAIR CONTRAST WITH THE GEOMETRIC LINES OF THE ROOM'S ARCHITECTURE. SIMILARLY, THE GENTLY UNDULATING HEADBOARD BRINGS A TOUCH OF SOFTNESS.

ABOVE: Creative thinking transformed this tiny room into a cozy haven in which small dimensions are not a liability but an opportunity. The bed has been tucked into the alcove, then dressed in vintage linens—Amish quilted pillow shams and a "Rob Peter to Pay Paul" quilt—creating a lively, colorful focal point for the room.

NO ROOM FOR A BEDSIDE TABLE? A CHEST CAN HOLD READING MATERIAL, WHILE A LAMP CAN BE MOUNTED TO THE WALL ABOVE THE BED.

A B O V E : A few unique touches can bring personality to a previously undistinguished room. A visit to the flea market might yield some special finds, such as this weathered bedside table and iron bed which contrast with the modern bedding and quilts and give this room a cozier, warmer feeling. The whimsical bedside lamp completes the transformation.

A B O V E : The addition of an eye-catching headboard treatment is a foolproof way to add excitement to a bedroom. Here, a romantic sweep of fabric is topped by a "crown," creating a royal backdrop for this bed.

Mattress Basics

If your mattress is not comfortable, the most beautiful room in the world will not help you get a good night's sleep. The standard bed set consists of a mattress and a box spring. Here is what you need to know before buying:

SIZE Mattresses come in four standard sizes: twin (39 x 75 inches), full (54 x 75 inches), queen (60 x 80 inches), and king (76 x 80 inches). Other sizes include toddler or crib, (usually 28 x 52 inches), and California King (74 x 84 inches).

COMFORT This is the top layer, the foam and/or fibers used in the upholstery layers above the innerspring.

INNERSPRING The innerspring is the support layer, with tempered steel coils that provide the system characteristics of the mattress. The number and arrangement of the coils and the wire thickness (or gauge) determine how much support the innerspring offers and its ability to evenly distribute weight. More coils and thicker wire (lower gauge means thicker wire) usually mean better support.

FOUNDATION The box spring, or the base of the sleep set, provides support for the mattress or comfort layer. The best way to purchase a box spring is as part of a set with a mattress. Don't mix and match an old mattress with a new box spring or vice versa.

Other choices in bed sets include:

FUTONS Usually made of cotton, but occasionally foam or synthetic fibers, futons are designed to be folded up during the daytime, either for storage or as seating. They frequently rest on a wooden base that folds down to make a sleeping platform but can also rest on a box spring.

FOAM MATTRESSES Made of latex rubber, polyurethane foam, or viscoelastic material, these mattresses (brands include TrueSleep and Tempurpedic) are made of a dense foam that is energy absorbing, heat sensitive, allergy resistant, and self-adjusting to body mass and temperature. Any of these options can be placed on a platform bed or box spring for the foundation layer.

WATERBEDS Basically a water-filled vinyl sack, waterbeds are nonallergenic. The newest waterbed designs have a water-filled core providing the support and layers of upholstery for insulation and surface comfort. They rest on a wooden frame. Quality construction is particularly important, so be sure to get the best quality.

LEFT: One wonderful piece of furniture, treated as a focal point, can give a room an entirely new feeling. Here, an iron bed with graceful, tulip-like curves provides this otherwise sparsely furnished bedroom with its own special character. A highlight of the mix of bed linens is a 1940s coverlet. The result is a bedroom with quiet but undeniable flair.

ONE-OF-A-KIND ACCESSORIES, SUCH AS THE VINTAGE BAKELITE RADIO, ADD PERSONALITY, PARTICULARLY WHEN ALLOWED TO STAND ALONE WITHOUT COMPETITION FROM OTHER ITEMS.

A B O V E : By mixing traditional details, such as the wooden rocker, the dresser, and the chandelier, with sleek Roman blinds and modern elements such as a small television mounted on the wall, this room got a modern makeover without losing its sense of old-fashioned comfort.

ABOVE: This simple room received a welcome dash of personality thanks to the clever combination of flea-market finds. Picket fencing makes a fun headboard that establishes a sweet country theme, further emphasized by the unframed amateur landscapes on the wall.

RIGHT: Arrange cherished items together to create a personal mix and enjoy the charming results, as in this bedroom. Note the combination of a modern quilt with hand-embroidered antique French linens, the etched-glass hurricanes with the freshly-painted 1940s dresser, and the vanity bench—picked up inexpensively at a flea market—with the 1890s hooked rug. These confident combinations result in a comforting aesthetic.

IF YOU FALL IN LOVE WITH A FLEA-MARKET FIND BUT FEAR THAT IT WON'T WORK IN COMBINATION WITH OTHER ITEMS, CONSIDER USING IT OUT OF CONTEXT AS A KIND OF FOUND ART—AS IN THIS WROUGHT-IRON FENCING AND FRENCH CANDELABRUM.

Let There Be Light

All too often overlooked in the planning stages, light is essential in creating ambience. Although you may not be ready to hire a lighting designer to create a custom lighting plan for your bedroom, by understanding the main principles of lighting design, you can make choices that will serve your design needs. Lighting comes in three categories:

AMBIENT, or general, overall light that illuminates an entire room. In daylight hours, the main source of ambient light is often the windows; in the evening, it frequently comes from an overhead fixture. For the bedroom, which rarely benefits from a bright, overhead light, some attractive ambient lighting solutions include recessed lighting, chandeliers or romantic pendants that do not create glare, and sconces or other wall-based lights.

TASK lighting shines brightly on specific areas used for work. If you read in bed, you'll want task lighting that is bright enough to illuminate your book, but not so bright that it fools your brain into thinking it's daytime. Table lamps or wall-mounted reading lamps that can be adjusted for angle are the best choices.

ACCENT lighting is intended to highlight a specific feature in a room, such as a painting or plant. Recessed downlights, spotlights, and uplights are all good choices.

When thinking about a room makeover, remember that a simple change in lighting can have a profound effect on the feeling of a room. The right combination of ambient, task, and accent lighting can create a sense of drama, romance, tranquillity, or even a combination of effects, depending on the nature and placement of the lights you select.

A B O V E : A rustic setting gets a modern update in this room. The bright daylight and natural beauty outside are maximized by simple, tab-top sheers on the windows behind the bed; the side window needs no covering at all. For nighttime, glass-topped lamps lend a touch of old-fashioned charm while ceiling- and wall-mounted halogen spots provide brighter illumination. Fresh linens in a mix of prints dress the bed invitingly.

LEFT: A collection of Hudson River School paintings provided the inspiration for the rich color scheme in this room. A mahogany sleigh bed and slip-covered chair bring the feeling forward from the nineteenth century to a more modern era.

ABOVE: In a sparsely decorated room with white walls, a new seagrass rug and a brushed metal bed make the vintage dressmaker's form and antique trunk become dramatic accents—a wonderful example of how the creative conjunction of old and new can express your personal vision in a truly unique way.

IN A ROOM WITH HIGH CEILINGS, PAINTINGS CAN BE STACKED ONE ABOVE THE OTHER, RATHER THAN PLACED SIDE-BY-SIDE. IT'S AN UNEXPECTED ARRANGEMENT THAT GIVES THE ROOM A FRESH FEELING AND ALSO DRAWS THE EYE UPWARD.

Transforming with Color

Color can influence mood and evoke eras, seasons, and places very clearly—which means that adding color is one of the most effective, quickest, and least expensive ways to refresh a room. There are many ways to utilize color for creating a change, from the most common—painting or papering the walls—to the more subtle, but still evocative—adding color in the form of accessories, trim, or details.

When choosing a wall color for the bedroom, decide first on whether you want a room that is soothing or stimulating. (Though it may seem counterintuitive to choose a stimulating color for a room you are going to sleep in, you can tone down the effect with lighting, so if you really want a vivid red boudoir or a sunny yellow nursery, go for it.) Generally, the tranquil side of the color palette includes all the pastels and neutrals, though you can work with a more intense shade if you use it sparingly. The stimulating shades generally are the more saturated colors.

Next, if there are aspects of your bedroom's architecture that need help, there are ways to visually improve it with color. Generally, a small or dark room can be visually enlarged or brightened with a light color; a large room can be made more intimate with a darker shade. To make a long, narrow room seem wider, you can paint the short walls in a dark shade, and the long walls in a lighter one. If your room has very high ceilings, painting the walls only three-quarters of the way to the ceiling line can make the ceilings seem lower to create a cozier atmosphere. Likewise, if you paint the wall up to the ceiling line, including the molding, you can make a low ceiling seem slightly higher.

LEFT: Decorator, know thyself: while some would find this pastel diamond pattern on their bedroom walls daring, pairing it with a yo-yo bedspread and a crocheted cover over the vanity bench is a choice others would call inspired.

A B O V E : Amish and Mennonite quilts provide the color in this master bedroom. The neutral walls are a terrific backdrop for the exquisite textiles, including the log cabin quilt from 1880 on the bed and the mid-nineteenth-century appliquéd oak leaf variation folded on the blanket chest.

ABOVE: The sunny yellow walls in this south-facing room enhance its natural warmth and give it a bright, lively feeling. Don't be afraid to break the rules: in this case, a vivid color is just the thing to give a small room a big personality without cluttering it with fussy details.

NOTE THE YELLOW DIAMOND PATTERN OVER THE DARK-STAINED FLOORBOARDS, A DETAIL ECHOED HIGH ON THE WALLS BY THE YELLOW FAUX-MARBLE FINISH ON THE CROWN MOLDING, UNDERLINED WITH A NARROW BAND OF BLUE-GRAY.

The Power of Color

Colors have widely varying meanings and effects on mood: Here are some feelings and associations typically linked with certain colors. You might feel differently about some of these colors, so trust your instincts.

STIMULATING	NEUTRAL OR VARIABLE	SOOTHING
RED Active, passionate, sensual.	**BROWN** Masculine, stable, earthy.	**PALE YELLOW** Calming, refreshing, cheering.
MAROON/PURPLE Royal, elegant, rich.	**DARK GREEN** Elegant, calming, quiet.	**PALE GREEN** Soothing, healing, tranquil.
RUST/GOLD Autumnal, warming.	**DARK BLUE** Serious, quiet.	**SOFT BLUE** Calming, restful, cool.
ORANGE Energizing, creative.	**WHITE** Pure, clean, innocent.	**LAVENDER** Romantic, nostalgic.
BRIGHT YELLOW Sunny, cheering.	**BEIGE** Earthiness, tranquillity, simplicity.	**PINK** Girlish, romantic, calming.
BRIGHT BLUE Youthful, vivid, mildly stimulating.	**BLACK** Formal, mysterious, strong.	**IVORY** Serene, calming, restful.

LEFT: Inspired by a trip to Tuscany, this room's décor was transformed by a rich palette of yellow, orange, and red tones. Stripes create a stunning setting for an eclectic mix of furnishings. A canopy of mosquito netting over the bed adds a touch of exotic romance.

ABOVE: This room was decorated in shades of muted green, blue, and yellow to create a tranquil yet stylish atmosphere. A mix of textures—seagrass, wicker, velvet, wool, linen, and damask—adds tactile interest while enhancing the feeling of comfort.

RIGHT: This bedroom evokes the feeling of a beachfront villa. Turquoise walls are reminiscent of the sea and sky, while the bright white of the bed sheets and draped headboard create an island of tranquillity amid the blue.

A SPECIAL PIECE CAN CREATE A FOCAL POINT FOR A ROOM. THIS SIX-PANEL SCREEN, UPHOLSTERED IN DAMASK, IS AN INTRIGUING TAKE ON A HEADBOARD; NOTE THAT ALL BUT ONE OF THE PANELS ARE ATTACHED TO THE WALL, MAKING THE LONG WIDTH FEEL MORE INTIMATE.

ABOVE: Wallpaper offers an enormous variety of decorative choices
and can determine the character of a room all by itself. In this cozy
attic room, vintage wallpaper in a pink rose print and caned twin beds
from the 1940s provide a flowery summertime look even when the
view from the balcony says otherwise.

A B O V E : It took courage to paint this room's slanted ceiling lavender, but the exquisite results should eliminate all doubt about the color choice, which is repeated in the upholstered headboard and wallpaper with its lilac trellis pattern. The yellow upholstered bench picks up a secondary color from the paper.

The Versatility of White

White lends itself to every decorating style. It can be modern, romantic, or traditional, depending on how it is used. The two main elements to think about when decorating with white are tone and texture. Tone will determine the underlying mood of your room; texture will provide interest. Here are a few ideas to consider:

White is not a single color, but rather a range, from soft, warm white (look for ivory or beige tones) to cool, bright white (look for gray undertones), as any trip to a paint store will reveal. If you are opting for white walls, think about the effect you want before choosing your paint or paper.

White-on-white decorating allows you to layer different shades and textures of white within a unified scheme. Consider using a variety of different fabrics, from cotton to lace to wool, and combining them in a range of tones. A mix of textures, from smooth to shaggy to rough, also makes for interesting effects. The result will be at once soothing and pleasing to the eye.

White is a wonderful way to unify disparate elements, such as flea-market or vintage furniture finds from different eras or styles: painted white, they can all cohabit happily. Similarly, a collection of white pottery on a white shelf presents a soothing tableau.

RIGHT: A white-painted room can be dramatically altered quickly and easily simply by changing the accessories. Here spots of bright color provide excitement against the white backdrop. The vibrant turquoise and strawberry red of the handmade bedstead are played up by the trim, curtains, folded quilt, and throw rug.

DRAMATIC ARCHITECTURAL ELEMENTS STAND OUT WHEN THE REST OF THE ROOM IS KEPT SIMPLE.

ABOVE: Inspiration for a change can come from a single element. Here, a simple sisal rug inspired a new wall color in this calm bedroom. Contrasting white trim on the window frame and attached shelf, plus a white ceiling, help reflect more light into the room.

RIGHT: The circa 1860 light-green cupboard is a classic that works well in this bedroom, grounded by the choice of deep-gray walls and white trim. The gray walls also serve to highlight the carved wooden panels salvaged from an Iowa farmhouse that hang above the circa 1875 iron bed.

Make a Quick Change

BE CREATIVE WITH PAINT

If you'd like to add a bold color to your décor—but you're not ready to paint an entire room—consider painting just one wall. It will make a splash without over-powering the room. You can reinforce the color throughout the room with accessories.

- Choose a new shade for the trim—a quick change that makes a substantial difference.

- Try a faux finish to add pattern or texture to a flat, boring wall. Sponging, ragging, combing, and color-washing are all easy, do-it-yourself projects, and many paint manufacturers make special products and offer instruction on how to do each one.

- Don't forget the ceiling—you'll be staring up at it from your bed, after all. If you use a paler shade of the wall color, it will create a soft glow. Using the same color on walls and ceilings results in a cozy, enclosed feeling. If you are feeling adven-turous, try something more playful—blue with clouds, a lightly stenciled pattern, or even a mural.

ABOVE: Neutrals need not be lacking in warmth, as this deep taupe shows. It provides a restful backdrop for the mix of early American textiles with their contrasting patterns and prints.

A B O V E : While gray may not be a common choice, it contrasts well with other colors and can have beautiful effects. The light and dark hues of the grays and whites in this bedroom are reminiscent of an old tinted photograph. The classic, traditional ambience is enhanced by the candle in the wall sconce—and the lack of any visible electric outlets or appliances.

PERFECTLY PRESERVED
ORIGINAL MOLDINGS
AND MANTELPIECE
SHOW A REVERENCE
FOR THE PAST.

EMPHASIZE DETAILS OF
TRIM BY PAINTING THEM
IN A CONTRASTING COLOR.

ABOVE: A simple coat of paint can have transformative powers. This bedroom has become vibrant and cheerful with its bright colors of marigold, red, and cornflower blue, all echoed in the quilt.

LEFT: Yellow walls are the key to making this room cheery and fun. The sunny wall color works well with the bright bedcover and rug. A chalkboard table at just the right height provides a place to express childhood creativity, while the flowers in pressed-tin frames along the wall offer inspiration to the young artist.

Keeping the Peace

Sometimes after all the stimulation of the day, what you really long for is a space that offers utter simplicity and peacefulness. The key to transforming your bedroom into a tranquil haven is to first know what you find to be peaceful—soft colors or perhaps no color at all? An absence of noise or visual stimulation? The inclusion of natural elements? Open spaces with no clutter? A nest with just a few cherished objects or pictures? Give some thought to what makes you feel truly relaxed, then bring in those elements.

The bedrooms in this chapter are perfect examples of soothing environments, created in a variety of interesting ways. Time-tested methods for achieving a sense of peace in a room include the liberal use of white or neutral shades; a spare, carefully edited choice of furnishings, an absence of clutter; and the use of natural fabrics and accessories. Many home decorators will also invite nature into the room by emphasizing views or adding plants.

Don't forget lighting and storage, two important elements in the quest for peacefulness. Soft, indirect lighting will go a long way toward creating a gentle feeling in a room. Sheers will filter daylight and provide privacy, while lamps and sconces will reduce harsh overhead lighting at night. Clutter is not restful. To make your bedroom a truly peaceful refuge, artfully display the objects you love and eliminate all unnecessary items.

L E F T : Wherever you reside, you can bring the charm of a country cottage to bear with whitewashed walls, linens from homespun and ticking, and soft pillows. While the décor may not make traffic sound like a babbling brook, it will certainly evoke a simpler time—without ever seeming dated.

ABOVE: Nature reigns in this room with wood, natural fibers, and seasonal flowers from the garden combining to create an indoor sanctuary. The no-frills approach to window treatments and bed linens allows the sculptural lines and textures of the furnishings to stand out to their best advantage.

LEFT: Varying textures in neutral shades create visual stimulation without overwhelming the senses, ensuring that a neutral color scheme needn't look boring. The variety of textures and fabrics in this room is unified by a cloudlike color palette that evokes serenity.

GOOD EXAMPLES OF CONTRASTING TEXTURES ARE THE LACY PILLOW-CASES AND KNITTED THROW ON THE BED AS WELL AS THE FLUFFY AREA RUG PLACED OVER THE TEXTURAL SISAL-LIKE CARPET.

ABOVE: Contrasting textures and a subtle range of colors give this bedroom its stylish comfort. Old and new come together gracefully in the weathered side table, tailored matelassé bed skirt, unfussy damask and linen pillow shams, and antique crocheted afghan. Nature makes an appearance in the seashells set in the glass cup on the table, and flower-filled bud vases on both sides of the bed.

THESE DREAMY WAFTING CURTAINS ARE MADE OF DOUBLE LAYERS OF WISPY VOILE. THE EXTRA LAYER ADDS BODY TO THE CURTAINS, SO THAT THEY BILLOW, RATHER THAN FLY AWAY, IN THE BREEZE.

The Beauty of Neutral Colors

A neutral palette is by nature a soothing color scheme—and therefore an excellent choice for a room that is meant to be relaxing. Neutral is far from dull. As a decorating palette, it is far from limited to variations of beige. Neutral encompasses both white and black, as well as their offspring, gray; the entire range of earth tones from ivory through taupe to chocolate; and it can also include pastels, if kept to shades of single hue. The key to creating a successful neutral color scheme is to work in a range of complementary tones, always keeping the effect subtle. As with white, remember to include variations in texture. Here are some tips from neutral territory:

1. Neutrals come in warm and cool shades, depending on the undertones. For example, yellow, apricot, or pink undertones lend neutrals warmth, while gray or blue undertones will lend coolness—choose your palette with this in mind.

2. When you have established your basic palette, you can mix and match all kinds of shades until you achieve the results you want.

3. Lush textures and trims are elegant in neutral shades, so feel free to experiment with voluptuous fringes, plump tassels, voluminous draperies, or other accessories that might seem overpowering in a brighter shade.

4. In a neutral color scheme, patterns can play a larger role allowing you to mix prints with impunity. Try varying patterns on the bed linens, floor coverings, curtains, and upholstery. A collection of throw pillows in the same prints will create unity.

5. Neutral fabrics are perfect for layering—try a mix of textures, such as a silk coverlet and a matelassé bedskirt or a wool wheat-colored carpet topped with a nubby multi-toned bedside runner.

When you decide to go with neutrals, remember that a well-designed neutral room is subtle and understated but never boring—the beauty lies in the details.

A B O V E : White walls aren't the only way to create a serene room. The pistachio color on the walls of this room is a hand-mixed hue that plays beautifully against the tea-dyed rose-strewn quilt that dresses the bed. Matching your paint colors to nature's calming palette can make an ordinary space extraordinary.

L E F T : This appealing bedroom uses white cotton in a variety of textures to create a welcoming oasis. The white sheets and cotton slipcovers on the headboard and footboard as well as the matching fabric-covered lamps provide a soft contrast to the natural pine walls. Campstools with tufted white cushions at the foot of the bed add to the "rustic chic" décor.

ABOVE: Here, a Mission-style bed grounds the room in tradition, while the buttery yellow walls, bedspread with scalloped edges, and diaphanous curtains keep the furniture from seeming too heavy.

RIGHT: This room eschews frills for a pared down yet unabashedly feminine look. A pastel palette and just a few pretty touches are the key to achieving this sweetly serene feeling: Note the ruffled edge on the pink bedcovers, and the unlined linen curtains which are ruched like the smocking of a dress. The pièce de résistance is the wonderful chandelier just dripping in crystals.

How to Soundproof a Bedroom

If your bedroom is large, your walls are thick, or you live alone down a country lane, you probably don't have a problem with noise. For everyone else, here are a few simple tricks for keeping intrusive noises to a minimum.

1. Carpeting or rugs on the floor are your first line of defense—they will muffle footsteps and any noise coming up from below. There is no need for wall to wall (unless you'd like it), but the larger and thicker the rugs, the more they will dampen noise within the room.

2. If noises are coming from neighboring rooms, apartments, or houses, consider lining your adjoining walls with cotton batting, cork tiling, or other soundproofing material. Shelves and bookcases might also help. There are soundproofing specialists you can hire for help if you do not want to do the work yourself.

3. If the noise is coming from above, don't resort to banging a broomstick on the ceiling, which never works for long and makes for bad neighborly relations. Instead, line the ceiling with soundproofing materials, and drape it with fabric. Again, consult a professional if the job seems too big.

4. Finally, if you are being assaulted by noise from outdoors, be it traffic or loud birdsong, consider replacing old windows with new, insulated types. In addition, thickly lined floor-to-ceiling drapes can cover not just windows but also walls. For an exterior line of defense, plant a barrier of evergreens along your property. As they mature, their thickening greenery will muffle street noise while providing attractive new views from every window in the house.

THIS FLOATING CANOPY CREATES A DRAMATIC EFFECT, BUT IT'S ALSO EASY TO MAKE. THE FABRIC IS STRETCHED ACROSS A THIN WIRE WHICH IS SECURED TO THE CEILING WITH TINY CUP HOOKS, AND IS ATTACHED TO THE BED FRAME WITH VELCRO. THIS MAKES IT EASY TO TAKE OFF AND WASH AT ANY TIME.

LEFT: Fantasy elements can bring a special feeling to a bedroom that makes it seem far from daily reality. Here an organza canopy gives an unpretentious wooden bed fairy-tale proportions. A box-pleated bed skirt grounds the confection with a more tailored touch.

ABOVE: A canopy is an excellent way to add a feeling of coziness, especially to a grand bed. It can also create a sense of separation from the day's hustle and bustle. In this room, rather than cover the entire top of the king-sized four-poster bed, a dramatic effect is achieved by loosely draping a length of fabric above the headboard.

RIGHT: Instead of a fully flounced canopy, this four-poster is curtained at either end in vintage lace panels and hand-crocheted strips. The various shades of off-white, beige, tan, and cream are inspired by a collection of seashells just visible in the top of a corner cupboard. The result is a bed that feels like a personal sanctuary.

Past Perfect

If you would like your bedroom to offer an escape from the pressures of modern life, think about making it a window to a time gone by—create a period room or one with enough vintage elements to make you feel like you've stepped back in time. If you have an older home, you may simply be continuing a theme that already characterizes your general décor; if not, it's fine to have a bedroom that's decorated unlike any other room in the home.

In deciding how to approach your décor, think about the styles that characterize different eras and which appeal most to you. Are you a fan of a rustic, early American style? Or perhaps you're a Victorian at heart, at home among exotic collectibles and floral patterns? Maybe it is the shag rugs and lava lamps of the 1970s that make you feel most comfortable? Another way to approach this decision is to build a room around a particular piece, such as an antique wedding chest from the 1880s. There is no need to re-create a museum-perfect replica of a period room; simply let a particular piece or time inspire you and choose elements that you feel work together.

If you have a flea-market browser's collection of cherished finds from several different periods, don't feel constrained to pick one—an eclectic room that contains elements from different eras can be just as charming. You can bring unity to the decorative scheme in other ways, such as using a particular palette or focusing on a theme. Then step out of your modern world into the past, and relax.

LEFT: The simple, unadorned beauty of the Shaker aesthetic has long been acknowledged as emblematic of peaceful comfort. Bright white walls provide the perfect background to highlight this gentle appeal, allowing the subtle homespun colors of natural dyes to stand out. Painted baskets and traditional quilts lend personality to the room. Above the bed an old interior gate with heart-shaped cutouts quietly asserts the integrity and longevity of handmade goods.

ABOVE: A perfectly preserved antique bed may be hard to find, but some creativity can fill in what is missing. Here, the posts from a Sheridan campaign bed of the early 1800s were found at an antique shop. The owner then hired a furniture-maker to recreate the base and canopy—a delightful mix of old style and new ingenuity, with a comfortable and authentic result.

RIGHT: This bedroom in a 1793 home evokes the Colonial era with its hearthstone fireplace, paneled walls, and wide-plank wooden floors. The four-poster bed is dressed in a checked canopy with deep folds of drapery recalling an earlier era yet appealing to modern tastes as well. The white cotton matelassé bed cover under a deep blue throw picks up color from the Delft tiles of the fireplace surround.

ABOVE: Before hooked rugs landed on the floor, they were actually made by Colonial-era settlers as bed coverings. This antique rope bed showcases a beautiful example, sewn in 1801 and featuring bold colors and a motif of vines and flowers. Vintage needlework also graces the wall and a footstool, bringing unity to the room's décor.

Test the Durability of Vintage Linens

Flea markets and secondhand stores are great places to pick up antique sheets for a song. Here are a couple of tricks to test the quality of sheets:

1. Hold up a sheet to the light to determine its quality. Light will not shine through a high quality sheet.

2. Higher quality sheets will not have fuzz or pills. You can test this by scratching the sheet with your fingernail to see if any lint comes off. If so, this is a sheet of lesser quality.

3. Obvious damage, such a tears, unraveling thread, or threadbare spots mean "do not buy."

L E F T : A mid-nineteenth-century rope bed is the centerpiece of this simple yet evocative room. An antique quilt dresses the bed, while a vintage hooked rug hangs over it.

RIGHT: This bedroom re-creates an eighteenth-century period Swedish summerhouse with vintage architectural elements, antique furniture, tea-stained fabrics, and carefully selected accessories. From the wooden shutters to the mix of striped and floral fabrics, every detail brings a sense of history and romance to the room.

THE LIGHTING IN THIS ROOM EVOKES AN EARLIER ERA WHILE STILL BEING FUNCTIONAL: THE CHANDELIER OVERHEAD PROVIDES AMBIENT LIGHT AS WELL AS ATMOSPHERE, WHILE THE VINTAGE LAMP ON THE MARBLE-TOPPED TABLE OFFERS A SOFTER, SECONDARY LIGHT SOURCE. NOTE ALSO HOW THE CANDLESTICKS AND WALL SCONCE REPEAT THE CANDLE MOTIF OF THE CHANDELIER.

A B O V E : Antique furnishings need not come from the same era to work well together. Here a Chippendale-style chest and a scroll-top mahogany stool coexist in harmony with a reproduction pencil-post bed. The pieces blend seamlessly because the rest of the room is simple, allowing the furnishings to cohabit comfortably.

L E F T : A vintage bed in tiger maple (also known as curly maple and prized for its unusual grain) is the centerpiece that gives this room its stately style. Bedding in tones of olive and red adds to the period feel. The deep, warm colors and period-style furniture contrasts beautifully against the bare pine board walls and floors.

A B O V E : A Victorian-style bedroom offers simple comforts with white bed linens, a tea-stained cotton duvet cover, and an antique accent pillow. The botanical prints above the headboard reveal the Victorian propensity for classifying and preserving nature.

L E F T : Architectural elements drawn from the past are excellent for projecting an old-fashioned ambience. Here, classic beadboard paneling acts as a historic backdrop to an acorn-topped four-poster bed. A collection of straw hats hanging off pegs on the wall contributes a fashionable note from days gone by.

Auction Advice

Auctions are terrific places to find unique items, often at bargain prices. Here are some tips to make your auction attendance more productive:

1. Arrive early to preview the items up for bid. Look them over carefully and note their size and condition.

2. At your first auction, spend some time just watching and learn how the process works. Don't worry about missing anything; there are sure to be plenty of items auctioned later on that you will be interested in.

3. Before you can bid, you'll need to register at the office to obtain a bidder number and card.

4. Always make your bids clear and precise so the auctioneer will understand whether you are bidding or not.

5. When the auctioneer says he is selling a piece "as is," it is usually damaged in some way. Keep that in mind when making your bid.

6. Know your budget limits—set them in advance—and never bid an amount of money you are unwilling to pay. Beginners may get caught up in the competition, and you don't want to get stuck buying something you do not truly want.

LEFT: This room draws its uncluttered charm from the built-in closet and drawers lining the wall. The café curtains allow light to enter, but still provide some privacy. In these pleasant, peaceful surroundings, a few choice period pieces—the iron bed frame, weathered garden bench, and Queen Anne chair—contribute to a pleasing mix.

ABOVE: A bedroom becomes a rustic retreat when furnished simply and authentically with a wagon wheel-patterned quilt topping a painted rope bed dating from the early 1800s. Rough floorboards are accented and softened by cotton rag area rugs.

LEFT: A collection of pint-sized chairs plus an antique rocking horse and game board make this re-creation of a child's room from the nineteenth-century at once authentic and accessible. The high four-poster bed has been dressed in curtains and a valance fashioned from old homespun fabric. A vintage-style quilt completes the picture.

NOTE THE PLACEMENT OF THE ANTIQUE FOOTSTOOL TO MAKE IT EASIER TO CLIMB INTO BED.

Updating the Look

Sometimes we want to draw from the past but not to recreate it; the goal is to let the past inform the present rather than overwhelm it. If we can bring beloved items into a more contemporary setting, the bedroom can be transformed into a personal haven that nevertheless makes a stylish and modern statement. The rooms in this chapter are contemporary and sleek, but often combine vintage and antique elements with modern furnishings for a more up-to-date spirit. This is an appealing approach for many of us who aren't ready for the demands of a period room, but still admire the workmanship, beauty, and evocativeness of pieces from the past.

Often, it is the manner in which antique objects are combined or displayed that makes them seem contemporary, as we show them in ways that never would have occurred to our forebears. Camp blankets, for instance, were for camping—not using in the bedroom. Similarly, a collection of stoneware vases would not have been displayed together on a tabletop, but either spread throughout the house or tucked away in a china closet where they would be protected. Another method for bringing a modern air to a room is to use color, pattern, and texture in ways that would not have been seen in the past. Old-fashioned fabrics such as toile, gingham, and cabbage rose can take on a surprisingly fresh look when presented in new ways.

Don't be afraid to experiment with combinations until you find the mix that makes your room work.

LEFT: Whimsy and a touch of humor go a long way toward updating country style. Here, white paint emphasizes this room's beadboard walls, while pastel shades on the bed covers soften the rustic feeling contributed by the exposed rafters. The fun is added in the form of a chrome bar stool used as a nightstand and a mounted trophy fish.

A B O V E : The contrast of antique elements with a bold black-and-white color scheme confers a confident modernity on this room. The custom-framed blocks of vintage-style black-and-white toile wallpaper hanging over the bed at once give a nod to the past and update the traditional pattern. Confined within frames, the toile can influence but not overwhelm the room.

BED LINENS OFTEN PROVIDE THE OPPORTUNITY TO BRING IN MODERN ELEMENTS AS HERE, WITH THESE LUXURIOUS HANDMADE QUILTS AND SHAMS, WHICH ARE FASHIONED FROM COTTON TOILE TO BE REVERSIBLE. THESE ARE ARTFULLY COORDINATED WITH SATIN SHEETS OF EGYPTIAN COTTON WITH THE SIMPLEST EDGING OF RICKRACK.

Choosing the Right Pillow

What type of pillow do you need? The answer lies in your preferred sleep position.

BACK SLEEPERS require firm support under the neck, but a gentle cradle under the head, so the pillow should be firm on the ends, but soft in the center.

STOMACH SLEEPERS should have a pillow with soft sloping surface and tapered ends.

SIDE SLEEPERS need a pillow that has a raised and even sleeping surface, allowing improved neck alignment.

A B O V E : This room makes old items seem new by presenting them in a truly modern fashion, with a clustering of like objects and a focus on geometric form. The British colonial bed from Singapore originally had three iron sides, but—unfettered by tradition—the owners fearlessly adapted it to fit their needs with spectacular results.

RIGHT: Free from any urge to create a period room around this Federal tiger-maple bed, this room's creators had fun with color, pattern, and texture. Sand-textured cocoa walls, hand-stenciled palm trees, and a caned rosewood bench bring tropical flair to the floral-print quilts and home-spun mix of bold red stripes, toiles, and gingham checks.

A COAT OF WHITE PAINT OVER THE BRICK GIVES THE FIREPLACE A FRESH, MODERN LOOK.

ABOVE: Weathered comfort is the theme in this bedroom in which old pieces are treated with respect but not museum-like reverence. The sepia-toned architectural photographs and aging pen-and-ink drawings inspired the palette of brown and white. The bed—originally brass—was brought up to date with white paint and layers of light-brown bedclothes. The nightstand was fished out of an old barn and given a new life here.

LEFT: Layers of color soak up light in this bedroom, which is anchored by an exquisite oak California Mission bed. The photo of John Coltrane, leaning against the wall in an unusual placement, hints at the owner's love of jazz and explains the rhythmic structure in the warmly patterned bedcoverings.

Make a Quick Change

LAYERING IDEAS

For an extra touch of interest and a hint of color, layer a fringed or patterned blanket under the bed's mattress, so that the blanket's fringe—or clean, colorful edges—hangs neatly over the top of a crisp tailored bedskirt.

You can mix blankets, comforters, bedspreads, duvets, throws, and quilts—all on the same bed if you like—by choosing fabrics that complement one another and layering them. Use a bedspread or duvet as the main covering, then fold a favorite blanket or quilt at the end of the bed, adding a throw on top. Feel free to experiment according to the seasons and your need for warmth—or creative expression. A bench at the foot of the bed can hold coverlets not in use.

Use throw pillows to create interesting layers of color and texture on the bed—you can try new colors and combinations easily this way, and you will also create a cozy, inviting nest. If you have a comfy chair in the room, add some pillows there, too.

RIGHT: The venerable charm of beadboard takes on a newly modern feeling when paired with starkly simple elements carefully chosen and placed to emphasize their form. The plain slipcovered headboard and unfussy bedspread create an oasis of simplicity for the bed. The geometric rhythm inherent in the patterns of the checkerboard rug and paneled walls stands out when there is no other pattern to compete. The shapes of the bedside table, vintage lamp, and bench at the foot of the bed are similarly highlighted.

ABOVE: When a bedroom is small, as those in older homes often are, decorating techniques that have an enlarging effect can give the room a lofty, more modern spirit. Here, one wall was covered with open shelving, and a coat of white paint was applied to lighten up the entire room for an overall fresher feeling.

ABOVE: Country, antique, and modern elements mix beautifully in this romantic master bedroom. Purple toile brings a country accent to the padded headboard, bed skirt, and French-inspired upholstered chairs. The mantel is an adaptation of a Greek Revival style from the 1880s. The pair of modern leather-upholstered cubes resting at the foot of the bed can be configured for use as dressing benches, ottomans, or side tables.

RIGHT: A collector of vintage floral fabrics created this room, which celebrates an era gone by without attempting to re-create it. Different floral fabrics grace the chair, bed, and pillows, but complementary colors bring them together beautifully. Flea-market paintings contribute their own charm to the flowery theme, while the curvaceous iron bed adds its own distinctive accent.

Plants in the Bedroom

A simple plant on your bureau or windowsill may enhance more than your décor. Scientists at NASA were among the first researchers to demonstrate that ordinary potted plants absorb common household gases like formaldehyde, ammonia, and benzene—thereby improving indoor air quality. Some of the best plants for this purpose are the areca palm, bamboo palm, rubber plant, and English ivy.

L E F T : Combining modern materials, classic forms, and luxurious fabrics gives this room its uniquely contemporary blend. The bed in particular exemplifies the approach: it is modeled on a traditional American four-poster but is manufactured of sleek steel. A Thai silk panel draped over the bed makes a dramatic canopy. Simple, modern linens decorate the bed, with the exception of a pair of toile-covered pillows, which impart a hint of the traditional.

CUSTOM BLINDS ECHO THE CANOPY'S DRAPE, UNITING THE ROOM'S DIFFERENT ELEMENTS.

Express Yourself

Bedrooms, not generally on public view, may be considered an excellent opportunity for personal expression. The bedrooms in this chapter highlight that spirit. Each room possesses a uniquely personal sense of creativity, beauty, and individuality. Even if you have never thought of yourself as particularly artistic, the rooms in this chapter will give you ideas and inspiration for adding your own essential nature to your bedroom.

In deciding how to put more of yourself (and perhaps your partner or children) into the décor, think about your experiences, interests, or passions. Perhaps you have a collection to display—what could be more soothing to your spirit when drifting off to sleep than gazing at a group of objects you have lovingly collected one by one? Or it may be that you want to surround yourself with family photos or original art.

Another way to infuse your bedroom with your own unique spirit is to make or personalize some aspect of it: with a little effort, you could add your own touch to the furniture, the accents, or the bedclothes. If you are a needleworker, you might knit an afghan, piece together a quilt, or sew some lace or trim onto your pillow shams. If you have a workshop, you might want to make a night table or lamp. Perhaps you are a Sunday painter or amateur photographer, and your own artwork could be displayed. Even a simple arrangement of fresh flowers expresses who you are. And ultimately, it is the time and consideration you put into your room that will instill some of yourself into its décor.

LEFT: A single, cherished painting holds center stage in this bedroom in a place of honor above the bed. Clean white walls create a gallery-like background. A personal touch is found in the luxurious fabrics dressing the bed.

RIGHT: Nature lovers brought the outdoors inside in this room, which features a whitewashed, twig canopy bed. Floral prints on the bed, framed botanical specimens on the wall, and potted plants placed around the room complete the room's transformation into a magical indoor arbor.

THIS BED IS PLAYFUL AND PERSONAL WITH ITS LAYERING OF DIFFERENT PRINTS, INCLUDING STRIPES, CHECKS, AND FLOWERS, AS WELL AS A TOUCH OF LACE.

ABOVE: This room reflects both the home's architecture—traditional Pueblo—and its occupant's passion for collecting. The solid white-washed walls and exposed beams create the perfect backdrop for an eclectic mix of collections, including the lacquered wooden boxes from Mexico on the bureau. Into the mix have been added a late-1800s log cabin quilt, and four white-and silver-painted tramp art frames hanging over the corner fireplace.

A B O V E : A passion for flowers, and roses in particular, inspired the décor of this idyllic room. Like a field of flowers under a sunny sky, hues of pink, yellow, and blue are spread around the room. The roses on the nightstand mimic the roses in the oil paintings on the walls, personal creations of the bedroom's owner.

R I G H T : Much of the fun in flea-market shopping comes from finding funky or kitschy items. In this whimsical room, a chenille bedspread, pillow shams, and matching overhead lampshade are among the many collectibles brought together in a charming mix.

How to Salvage Old Stuff

Cast-off or battered furniture can make unique pieces for your home with a little ingenuity. Here are a few ideas:

• A table with a damaged top can be made good as new by replacing the top with a weathered door, a homemade mosaic tabletop, or a piece of custom-cut glass.

• A bucket or large pot with a hole makes an excellent planter—drainage already included.

• Fabric remnants from old quilts, curtains, rugs, or tablecloths can be sewn into one-of-a-kind pillow covers, curtains, wall hangings, or bedskirts.

• Mismatched, chipped old china can be broken up into mosaic pieces.

• Old tools, kitchen gadgets, or architectural bits—framed or simply hung on the wall—become works of art.

Make a Quick Change

You may not need a makeover; try a new window treatment and see what a difference it makes:

- Layer the fabrics covering your windows. A gauzy inner curtain of linen, muslin, or other sheer fabric will provide diffused, soft light and an airy feeling during the day. At night, a heavier overlayer will maintain your privacy.

- The top layer (or layers) of curtain can make a strong statement. Choose deeply colored velvet or heavy cotton drapes to transmit a rich, luxurious feeling; sunny yellow or bright green gingham curtains to create a country cottage ambience; a length of simple linen in a neutral tone to form a peaceful frame for an eye-catching view. Length also matters: short curtains are more casual than floor-length or puddled styles.

- Go for a clean look with blinds instead of curtains. The choices are wide, and custom blinds can be relatively inexpensive. Metal blinds can impart a stark, sophisticated modernity. Wooden blinds can be vintage, rustic, or country. Fabric shades, such as Roman blinds, are simple and modern, yet convey a softer feeling.

- If your view is spectacular and privacy is not an issue, consider no window treatment at all.

- If your view isn't pleasing, consider adhesive panels that attach directly to the windowpanes with a translucent yet obscuring pattern. They let in light but cover up the view.

RIGHT: If it is the artistic vision of someone else you admire, let it inspire you. The colors and sparse décor of this room are reminiscent of a Van Gogh oil painting, *The Artist's Bedroom*. Each of the elements was chosen in homage to the artist.

A B O V E : The patina of rust on this iron bed frame, coupled with floral bedding and white walls, create the illusion of a restful cottage bedroom. An antique doll crib adds another whimsical touch.

L E F T : The vivid colors and patterns of Navajo textiles set the design scheme for this bedroom. Note the wall hung 1930s Navajo rug that serves as a headboard. While these textiles are too precious for everyday use, a red wool hotel blanket visually unites the color story. Rustic accents—the wooden bench, tin-framed mirror, and painted metal box—reinforce the western theme.

RIGHT: Spacious but lacking in storage, this bedroom needed a unique solution to give it personality and function. The answer lay in adding a custom, freestanding armoire, which also created an interior wall for the bed to stand against. The armoire and bed were centered beneath the wooden support beam of the ceiling, creating a dramatic focal point for the room.

A BEAUTIFUL TRANSOM WINDOW SALVAGED FROM AN OLD BUILDING ENJOYS A NEW LIFE AS THE CENTER OF THIS HANDCRAFTED HEADBOARD.

ABOVE: A personal decorating stamp might come in the form of a love for a certain color. Here a brilliant yellow floor transforms a sparsely furnished bedroom into a sunny paradise. The panelled, cottage-style bed frame echoes the architecture in this cozy attic space.

A B O V E : While this bedroom just happens to open onto a porch in Hawaii with a view of the Pacific, with the proper elements any bedroom can capture an open and breezy feeling. Wide floorboards, white clapboard walls, and an unfinished ceiling suggest the spirit of ease and openness. Touches of color, like the turquoise window trim and the 1930s Hawaiian fabric quilt, add warmth, and the canopy of mosquito netting overhead creates an inviting refuge.

RIGHT: Even more than adults, children love to express their enthusiasm in their rooms—so why not encourage them? Pink-and-white stripes, checks, and ruffles give a sweet air to this room decorated for a young girl with a love for ballet. The rugs and walls were kept warm and neutral to create a sophisticated and flexible backdrop in case her affection for the color pink should change.

GROUPS OF BALLET-THEMED PRINTS ADORN TWO WALLS, WHILE A SET OF CERAMIC PLATES IS AFFIXED WITH RIBBONS TO THE WALL BEHIND THE BED—EXPRESSIVE YET EASILY CHANGED.

Make a Quick Change

KID'S ROOM FAST MAKEOVER IDEAS

Kids are famous for their ever-changing interests and moods. As they head toward the teen years, this grows more pronounced, along with a strong need to express themselves—and what better place than their room? Remember that a neutral background makes it easier to make quick changes in a room.

- Replace the bed linens: a new blanket, comforter, or duvet cover in a different color, pattern, or style can make it seem like a whole new room.

- Add a new accent color: use it for throw pillows, an area rug, easy-hang tab curtains, shelves, or paint one wall in the new favorite color.

- Create a place for personal expression: use cork tiles, a metal board with magnets, or a framed fabric-covered bulletin board for pictures, keepsakes, posters, and the like—it can take up as much wall space as you wish.

- Let the child participate in creating personalized accessories: try making a stamped paper lampshade, a painted window shade, an appliquéd pillow, or simply hang a collection of the child's own artwork in frames.

LEFT: Two clever elements make this room a perfect haven for someone whose interests change frequently. A simple wooden board with multiple hooks allows the enthusiasm of the moment to be displayed above the bed. Baskets can hold a multitude of items and—best of all—they can be stashed beneath the bed.

ABOVE: Kids are enthusiastic collectors—indeed, most adults who enjoy collecting started young. In this room, neutral colors and simple furnishings allow the objects on display to change easily. Cherished items, like the rusted cars, dog painting, bowling pin, and skates, can give way to new interests without having to change anything major.

AN OLD BURLAP POTATO BAG BECOMES AN AMUSING PILLOW FOR THIS TIME-WORN WICKER ROCKER.

RIGHT: A magnificent carved Victorian headboard is the focal point of this room, while the use of white is the unifying element, bringing together the wood paneling, headboard, and indoor/outdoor chairs and tables.

THE HALF-MOON WINDOW ECHOES THE SHAPE OF THE HEADBOARD; ALONG WITH THE HIGH CEILING, IT HELPS PREVENT THE HEADBOARD FROM OVERPOWERING THE ROOM.

A B O V E : Romantic and masculine needn't be opposites, and this room actually makes them a match made in heaven. It is the combination of cool colors and cozy textures that makes it work. Shades of blue, green, and brown, along with the metal lamps and vintage photos, are appealingly masculine, while an abundance of pillows, textured bedding, and fresh flowers soften the atmosphere enough to make it inviting.

R I G H T : What more romantic piece of furniture is there than a recamier? Its curvaceous lines recall a gentler era. The spirit of romance it brings to this room is extended by the ruffled treatment on the duvet and pillow shams, as well as the canopy of diaphanous mosquito netting. A bold color scheme of sunny yellow complemented by deep-blue violet adds sophistication.

Romantic Retreats

Why is a romantic bedroom such a delight to come home to? Perhaps because it allows us to emphasize the emotional aspect of our lives, which we often must repress during the busy efficiency of our days. Our bedrooms, after all, are not only places of privacy and self-expression, but also rooms in which we can relax and reveal our emotional selves.

The key to creating a romantic room lies in understanding your own definition of romance. It may be a confection of pleasing pastels and soft, flowing fabrics; a celebration of a gentler era gone by; a tranquil hideaway where harmony reigns; or a warm, sensual boudoir. Or it may be none of these, but a uniquely personal space where you feel happy.

Although each of us has our own idea of what is romantic, there are a few common elements all the rooms in this chapter share: an inviting air, a devotion to comfort, and a feeling of sensuousness. A sense of welcome not only entices us to enter a room, it also encourages us to stay there. Comfort is essential to true relaxation and should be a feature not only of the bed, mattress, and linens, but of the room as a whole. A sensuous room finds a way to indulge the senses, inviting us to luxuriate in the moment. These qualities add up to romance.

LEFT: A rich, warm palette gives this elegant room its sense of romance, while a subtle blend of textures adds sophistication. The warm sienna-colored walls and soft ivory curtains and bedding counter the rich, dark wood of the bed and night table. The floral rug repeats all the colors, bringing unity to the room. On the bed, which is nestled cozily into the corner, is a collection of pillows in different textures, including leather—an unexpectedly masculine note that gives the room its distinctively sophisticated ambience.

RIGHT: This room has a quiet air of romance that comes from its combination of feminine details and cheerful comfort. Soft colors, like the buttery yellow that gives the room its sunny character, are light-enhancing and restful. Even the yellow slip becomes a romantic accent silhouetted against the sheer curtains.

MIXING STRIPES AND FLORALS IS A TIME-HONORED TRADITION; THE STRIPES HELP TO PREVENT THE FLORAL PATTERNS FROM BECOMING OVERWHELMING.

LEFT: French country florals provide a romantic theme for this pretty-in-pink (and blue) room. A mix of pink and red flowers and stripes stands out against the deep-teal walls, while a trio of vintage floral-printed cardboard trays add their own romantic charm.

Please the Senses

Though sight tends to take precedence, your bedroom should have something to please every sense:

- For complete darkness while you sleep, try lining your drapes with a new microfiber backing product or interlining, which allows them to fall more naturally than old-fashioned blackout lining. Hold samples up to the light and check how much light they block.

- To please your sense of touch, buy sheets with the highest thread count. Then, mix the fabrics on top of your bed for contrast—cotton, linen, wool, down, cashmere—whatever pleases you.

- Don't forget your sense of smell. Flowers, scented candles, and linen sprays can add a hint of sensual fragrance—a small touch that will have a pleasing effect.

- Create a personal soundscape in your room by adding a sound machine—you can choose from a variety of natural sounds or simply the soothing hum of white noise. A small but high-quality radio or stereo system will allow you to create your own musical accompaniment.

- Keep a special water carafe and glass next to your bed; why get out of your cozy nest just to quench a nocturnal thirst?

RIGHT: A canopy, which adds both coziness and drama, is always a romantic touch. In this bedroom, the entire room has been draped with muslin to create a totally luxurious setting. Since the entire room is canopied, the frame on the bed is left bare, becoming an elegant architectural ornament, just as the wooden pediment mounted on the wall above the frame.

IF YOU CANNOT FIND LINENS THAT YOU LIKE, OPT FOR CUSTOM LINENS. THIS HANDCRAFTED DUVET COMBINES THREE PANELS OF NEW INDIAN SILK BACKED BY A KING-SIZE SHEET.

ABOVE: A few well-chosen items make this bedroom personal, comfortable, and inviting. The painted Victorian bed is romantic in itself; adding a luxurious vintage eiderdown, sweet pink ruffled sheets, and a pile of pillows completes the picture.

LEFT: A grandly curvaceous headboard sets a romantic tone in this room. Delicate swirls on the bedside tables, echoed in the lamps, further emphasize the theme, while the contrasting mix of toile and floral-patterned bedding evokes a look of luxurious comfort.

Adapting an Armoire

It is fairly easy to adapt an armoire to hold a television, stereo, computer or other electronic equipment. Keep in mind that this kind of alteration would lower the value of an antique, so choose a piece that you like but that is not a venerable antique. The goal is to add the extra support and ventilation necessary to safely hold the equipment.

1. Measure each piece of equipment to see how deep it is and make sure it will fit inside and still allow the doors to be closed.

2. Measure the floor of the armoire and either replace or reinforce it with a piece of ¼-inch plywood.

3. Replace the original shelves with ¾-inch plywood, and install metal brackets or wooden supports to support the shelving.

4. Be sure to make cutouts at the back end of the shelves for cords to be threaded through.

5. Place the equipment in the position it will ultimately sit and mark on the armoire where you want the cords to emerge from the back, then cut the hole.

6. Avoid piling items atop one another: electronics need space around them for ventilation.

RIGHT: Sumptuous fabrics in a variety of textures, all linked by their floral motifs, give this room its sense of romance. A minor, but elegant note: tassels line the drapes and bed pillows.

ARMOIRES CAN CONCEAL A MULTITUDE OF OBJECTS AND ELECTRONIC DEVICES THAT MIGHT DISTRACT FROM YOUR DÉCOR. THIS ARMOIRE HIDES A TELEVISION—AN ITEM THAT WOULD SURELY LOWER THE ROMANCE FACTOR IF DISPLAYED OPENLY.

LEFT: The focus of this inviting room is the graceful four-poster cherry bed. Dressed in checked and floral linens, its scale establishes the very essence of early American romance—not to mention the ability to close it off with drapes on three sides.

RIGHT: The everyday comfort of this room is what makes it appealing. Clapboard walls and soft, scrim-like curtains create a pleasant environment in which a slip-covered easy chair fits right in. A Victorian cottage bed takes a turn for romance when the white sheets are turned down and the brightly colored floral bolster beckons.

Bed Sheet Basics

To slip between soft, clean, welcoming sheets is undoubtedly a great pleasure—why not give yourself that kind of treat nightly? Yet choosing new sheets can be a daunting task. What are the different fibers and how do they affect quality? What is thread count? Here's a quick primer on the main terminology used in describing sheets.

COTTON SHEETS are commonly found in three varieties: Egyptian cotton is considered the finest, then Pima, and then American Upland. Cotton sheets are the most breathable.

COTTON-POLYESTER sheeting, usually a fifty/fifty blend of cotton and synthetic fibers, is popular because it doesn't wrinkle and is less expensive than 100 per cent cotton.

LINEN sheets are the most expensive, but also the most breathable, and tend to last a long time.

THREAD COUNT refers to the number of threads per inch of fabric. A higher thread count means a tighter weave and a finer sheet. Top quality sheets have thread counts of 200 and higher.

PERCALE is a sheet with a minimum 180-thread count. Percale sheets may be cotton or cotton blends.

LEFT: In a room inspired by a collection of French antiques, a canopied daybed, draped in luxurious layers, sits beneath a low-hanging, crystal chandelier. The artful mix of linens includes crisp cotton on the bottom; a softer, diamond-quilted layer above; and a collection of pillows, all topped with a plush throw.

ABOVE: If you have the opportunity to combine two small spaces into a larger one, you can effect a major transformation. This spacious room, previously two small and inefficient rooms, now serves double duty as a romantic bedroom and light-filled sitting room. Simply furnished and awash in delicate florals and faded paisleys, the room has a relaxed ambience that is comfortable and welcoming. To take the best advantage of the space and light, a plump oversized chair is situated next to the wide windows to receive maximum daylight, while the bed is tucked against the far wall, a more cozy and private location.

Welcoming Guests

Many homes are spacious enough to have a special room set aside for visiting relatives, friends, and other guests. There is a temptation to fill the spare room with rejected pieces from other bedrooms, but you should resist! It is much nicer for you and for your visitors if the guest room is not a clutter of mismatched leftovers, but rather, has an identity of its own. Not only do your guests deserve comfort and tranquillity, but you will find it pleasing to have an extra room that is attractive.

Because it is not your own room, and may be used by many different people, it can be difficult to choose a design theme. The rooms in this chapter show how many opportunities there are to infuse a room with comfort, cleanliness, beauty, and a spirit of hospitality. One key element is storage. Storage that you keep empty and clean rather than filled with your own belongings is essential if your guests are to be able to unpack and set themselves up in relative comfort and convenience. The other important aspect of a good guest room is less tangible: a feeling that the room is a space in which your guest may relax and unwind, and claim the room, however briefly, as his or her own. Achieving this might be as simple as including a comfortable chair and ottoman, placing a selection of reading material on a shelf or nightstand, or including a small worktable or desk.

Think about what would make you feel at home in someone else's house and you will begin to grasp the essence of hospitality.

LEFT: Sparse furnishings and a lack of clutter add up to a peaceful room; in this case, it also has a sense of warmth that comes from the careful choice of furniture and fittings. The custom-made twin beds from the 1920s, graced with carved-narcissus finials, are pretty and inviting. Sheer-cotton Roman shades over each window provide privacy while permitting light to pour in, giving a glow to the pale buttercream paint that protects and preserves the old chestnut flooring.

LEFT: Fresh and nautical, this blue-and-white striped room offers a cheery welcome. While it isn't necessary to outfit every guest bed with a smiling teddy bear, it doesn't hurt to consider a bit of whimsy or a reminder of childhood to put someone at ease in new surroundings. Clean, crisp white linens are always welcoming, and the addition of an extra throw blanket or quilt at the foot of the bed is not only a great design accent, but a thoughtful way to guard against night chills.

ABOVE: Simplicity is invariably a good approach to a guest room. Here, white walls create a serene environment, a brass bed anchors the room while contributing a sculptural quality to the décor, and a handmade cotton quilt provides color. A bit of whimsy comes from the railroad lantern used as a bookend for a collection of well-worn favorites from the 1920s.

Making Guests Feel Welcome

A few thoughtful touches in the guest bedroom will ensure that your visitors feel welcome:

- A bedside table equipped with an alarm clock, a reading light, and a selection of reading material (books, recent magazines).

- Space in the closet and empty drawers in the bureau for their things.

- A table or desk and chair (a telephone is a nice extra).

- A welcoming vase of fresh flowers.

RIGHT: Fabulous vintage pillows and bedspreads come together in this charming guest room decorated in shades of green. A thoughtful touch is a pair of circa 1940 metal night-lights attached to the beds.

ABOVE: The charm of childhood playthings makes this room a delightful place to stay, no matter what the age of the guests. Matching yet not identical, each side is equipped with coat-rack shelves, and tables at the foot of the beds offer plenty of room for personal expression and practical storage.

ABOVE: Lots of kids—or grandchildren—but don't have several rooms to set aside for them? This large room solves the problem with three matching side-by-side four-poster beds, each identically dressed in cotton log cabin quilts. With a metal cabinet at the foot of each bed to hold personal objects, the effect is of a fun sleep-away camp, sure to please visitors of any age.

Make a Quick Change

MAKE A DUVET COVER

If the duvet or comforter cover of your dreams doesn't seem to exist, or if you are on a budget that limits your options, consider making your own duvet cover, which is essentially just a big bag to hold a duvet or comforter.

1. Purchase fabric of your choice or a couple of flat sheets in the right size for your bed.

2. Right sides facing, sew the sheets/fabric together on three sides.

3. Sew grommets, buttonholes, a zipper, or ribbon ties (depending on your style) to the fourth side.

4. Insert your comforter, and close. Voilà—a custom duvet cover.

LEFT: To create a warm feeling using a mix of patterns, start with a neutral backdrop and simple furnishings, as in this room. The blend of floral prints, madras plaids, gingham checks, calico cottons, and stripes of all widths and rainbow hues work together here to set a casual mood. The vintage suitcases are an appropriate theme for travelers, and several cot mattresses stored under the bed ensure a welcome for a group of any size.

ABOVE: A guest room that is simple, clean, and neutral is easy on the eyes and welcoming to guests of any stripe. In this room, the fresh, white sheets and covers with these matching antique Hungarian headboards offer a pleasant invitation to sleep. The soft texture of the waffle-weave coverlets and the quilted pillow shams soften the rugged, earthy texture of the exposed brick wall.

LEFT: Twin beds needn't be dressed identically; after all, even identical twins have slight differences that give them individuality. Guests will enjoy noting the differences, as in the twin beds in this room, which benefit from the interplay of like and unlike. Both beds have painted white metal frames, but each has a unique headboard. Such slight variations continue throughout the room, making for a varied and interesting design.

ABOVE: Guest rooms offer the perfect place to situate outstanding pieces that you love but feel might not work in a master bedroom. These twin wooden headboards painted with flowers are a wonderful example; they give this lovely room a fairy-tale feeling sure to enchant visitors. The duvet covers are new, but were created from a fabric whose old-fashioned feeling, color scheme, and pattern won't break the spell.

ABOVE: If neutral is not your style, perhaps you'd prefer to greet your guests with a room full of personality. Here, pastoral toile wallpaper in a mellow mix of olive and cranberry tones welcomes guests warmly into an old-fashioned room. The antique twin beds are swathed in a mix of floral sheets, handmade quilts, and plaid and check coverlets that would make any guest feel comfortable no matter what the temperature.

Comforters and Duvets

Although these labels tend to be used indiscriminately to refer to filled bed covers that don't go over the pillows, there are differences. Here is a primer:

- A duvet is a 100 per cent down-filled bed covering. The best quality duvets contain white goose down, which is the fluffy covering under the breast feathers of a goose or duck. Lesser quality duvets include regular feathers.

- When buying a duvet, look for a high "fill power"—or density—of at least 625 cubic inches, which means that the comforter will insulate well, but still be light in weight.

- A comforter is a bed covering that has polyester filling. These tend to be much less warm than down, so they work well in warmer climates and seasons. They often come in fashionable colors and prints, with matching accessories.

- Alternatives to down and polyester fillings do exist, but may be a bit harder to find. Look for fillings such as silk or wool instead.

- Look for "baffled construction," which means that fabric walls are stitched into the comforter's interior to prevent the filling from shifting.

LEFT: Blue and white is among the most popular of color pairings and is likely to make guests feel comfortable. This room's vintage pieces stand up well to the strong wall colors. The white whole-piece quilts and blue-and-white patchworks warm the Colonial Revival mahogany beds and lighten the strong effect of the intense color.

ABOVE: Side-by-side guest rooms allow for as much togetherness or privacy as guests might need, and a shared color palette brings them a sense of unity if the door is left open. A lovely gesture is to welcome guests with fresh flowers or plants—here, the paperwhites by the bed are a sweet reminder that spring is on the way.

A B O V E : This room's white walls, clean sisal rugs, and sturdy white pine furniture provide a perfectly neutral backdrop that is pleasant and comfortable for visitors of all ages. Colorful bedding that changes with the seasons makes it fun.

Photography Credits

Index